DATE DUE

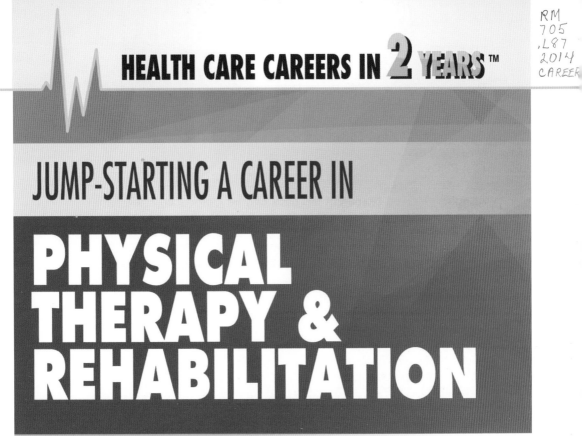

HEALTH CARE CAREERS IN 2 YEARS™

JUMP-STARTING A CAREER IN

PHYSICAL THERAPY & REHABILITATION

MARCIA AMIDON LUSTED

ROSEN
PUBLISHING®

New York

Published in 2014 by The Rosen Publishing Group, Inc.
29 East 21st Street, New York, NY 10010

Copyright © 2014 by The Rosen Publishing Group, Inc.

First Edition

Library of Congress Cataloging-in-Publication Data

Lusted, Marcia Amidon.
Jump-starting a career in physical therapy & rehabilitation/Marcia Amidon Lusted.—First edition.
    pages cm—(Health care careers in 2 years)
Audience: Grades 7-12.
Includes bibliographical references and index.
ISBN 978-1-4777-1695-3 (library binding)
1. Physical therapy—Vocational guidance. 2. Physical therapy assistants—Vocational guidance. 3. Occupational therapy—Vocational guidance. I. Title.
RM705.L87 2014
615.8'2023—dc23

2013013960

Manufactured in Malaysia

CPSIA Compliance Information: Batch #W14YA: For further information, contact Rosen Publishing, New York, New York, at 1-800-237-9932.

CONTENTS

INTRODUCTION

I t's eight o'clock in the morning and the physical
therapy assistant has just arrived at the physical
therapy department of a large hospital. There are
already patients in the waiting room. Some of them
have visible injuries, such as arms in slings, or use
wheelchairs or crutches. Others don't appear to be
injured. Some are elderly, some are young adults, and
some are children or teens. Some are seeking help with
injuries or the aftermath of surgery, while others are trying
to avoid having surgery.

The physical therapy assistant looks at the list of
patients for the day and reviews it with the supervising
physical therapist. Each returning patient has an established plan of care, developed by one of the physical
therapists on staff. The plan outlines what the patient's
physical problem is and how the therapists will treat that
condition. There is also a new patient on the list. She will
have an initial evaluation to determine her problem before
a plan of care is created.

The physical therapy assistant sets up the private area
where the first patient's therapy will take place. The assistant applies laser therapy to a sore muscle under the
supervision of the physical therapist, who then massages
it to loosen the muscle and alleviate the pain. The next
patient is treated in a large open room with equipment

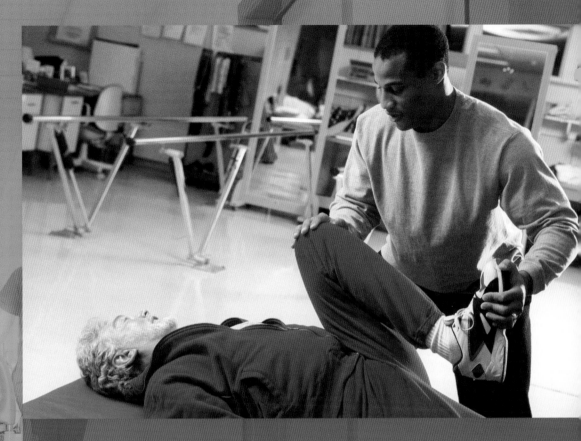

Physical therapy assistants help patients exercise limbs after injury or surgery.

such as weights, arm and leg bicycles, railings for assisted walking, and a small trampoline. This patient needs help exercising an injured leg that recently underwent surgery. The supervising physical therapist carries out this particular therapy, and the assistant documents everything that takes place in the patient's record on a laptop computer.

The next patient is new, and the supervising physical therapist conducts the evaluation of the woman's injury. The assistant enters information in the patient's record as the therapist does the evaluation and listens as the therapist and the patient discuss what treatments and procedures will be used to help her. They also discuss how frequently and for how long the patient will come in for treatment and what the patient's goals are for the therapy.

The end of the day comes quickly, and the physical therapy assistant, with the help of the physical therapy aide, cleans up the facility and gets it ready for the next day. When the assistant leaves at 5 PM, it is with the satisfaction of having spent the day helping people reach their therapy goals and feel better. All of this is possible with just two years of higher education.

Chapter 1

Exploring the World of Therapy and Rehabilitation

Physical therapy and its related career, occupational therapy, can be very appealing to those who want a steady, well-paying job that also involves helping people. What is the difference between the two? While both careers involve helping people regain physical strength or recover from a physical problem, each has a specific focus.

A Difference in Focus

Professionals in the physical therapy field work with patients who have had injuries, illnesses, or surgeries, or who have other disabling conditions. They may have lost movement in parts of the body, such as the arms, legs, or back. They may have been in an automobile accident or sustained a sports injury, or they may suffer from a condition such as cerebral palsy or arthritis. Some may be experiencing a physical condition that they are hoping to heal without surgery. These patients need help regaining movement and managing pain. Treatment might include

Equipment such as weights can help patients strengthen weak muscles.

exercise, massage, ultrasound or laser treatments, and heat or cold therapy.

Like physical therapy, occupational therapy helps people who have decreased physical mobility because of an illness, accident, injury, or surgery. However, the focus is on recovering the ability to perform everyday activities, rather than alleviating pain or healing the injury. An

SPEECH AND LANGUAGE THERAPY

There is another type of therapy career: speech and language therapy. Therapists called speech-language pathologists help patients with communication disorders, such as stuttering, difficulty pronouncing words clearly, or problems with pitch or tone. They also help people with swallowing disorders. Their patients may have receptive disorders (difficulty understanding what other people are saying) and expressive disorders (difficulty putting words together correctly or using language in a socially acceptable way). Jobs as speech-language pathology assistants or aides do exist, but regulations and requirements for these careers vary from state to state. Those interested in this field can learn more through the American Speech-Language-Hearing Association (ASHA), at http://www.asha.org.

occupational therapist also works with individuals with mental or emotional disabilities as well as physical ones. Overall, the goal of occupational therapy is to help people improve their quality of life by regaining the ability to do everyday tasks without assistance. These things might be as basic as the ability to bathe or cook for themselves.

Other patients might work on regaining skills for holding down a job after a work-related injury.

Like physical therapy, occupational therapy often includes physical movement, such as stretching and relaxing. However, it also includes hands-on skill building, such as learning how to move from a bed to a wheelchair or relearning how to cook in a simulated kitchen setting. Many occupational therapy facilities have simulated work and home settings in which patients can practice daily skills.

Getting Started: The Aide and the Assistant

There are several levels of careers in physical and occupational therapy. The first level is that of aide. Being a physical or occupational therapy aide does not require any higher education, only a high school diploma. For both types of therapy, aides perform tasks such as cleaning the therapy facility, setting up treatment areas, and helping patients move to and from their treatment area. Typically, aides are not involved in hands-on patient care. They might do clerical work, such as scheduling appointments and answering phones, or helping patients with insurance forms and billing.

Physical and occupational therapy assistants participate more fully in patient treatment. Physical therapy assistants may observe patients and report on their status to the physical therapist, help them with specific exercises, or apply massage, heat, or cold treatments. They may help patients with specific devices such as walkers. They might even educate a patient's family about what to do between treatments, such as showing them what exercises should be done at home. In addition, they record patient progress and keep their records updated. They may also encourage patients when necessary. In some therapy settings, a physical therapy assistant performs many of the actual therapy treatments under the supervision of the physical therapist. But in other facilities, they just assist the therapist.

Occupational therapy assistants help with therapeutic treatments such as stretching and other exercises, as well as recording patients'

Occupational therapy with children often incorporates toys and play activities.

progress and doing administrative work. They might work with disabled children, conducting play activities to promote coordination or movement. They might teach someone with arthritis or Parkinson's disease how to use special devices to make eating easier. An occupational therapy assistant may also help develop a patient's

A rehabilitation professional needs to be physically fit in order to move and support patients during activities.

treatment plan and then carry out many of the treatment activities. The amount of responsibility the assistant can take on varies in different therapy settings.

What Does It Take?

What are the necessary skills and abilities that a candidate must have in order to be a successful physical or occupational therapy assistant? Above all, the assistant must be responsible, capable of working without constant supervision, and willing to be a team player. Working directly with patients requires good people skills, such as the ability to listen and be sympathetic. An assistant must also be observant, paying close attention to what patients express both verbally and nonverbally, in order to keep accurate records and make helpful reports to the supervising therapist. The assistant must communicate well with other members of the therapy team, including the supervising therapist, office and administrative personnel, and referring doctors and their offices.

It is also important that an assistant be at least somewhat physically fit. Both physical and occupational therapy often involves helping patients move. This might mean lifting patients from a wheelchair to a table, or supporting people while they use railings to improve their walking. There is also a great deal of bending and stretching involved in many treatment activities. An assistant who is not able to move easily throughout an eight-hour workday will not be effective at assisting patients and may even damage his or her own health.

AN AGING WORLD

Job opportunities in physical and occupational therapy are growing at a faster rate than in many other careers. As the U.S. population ages, there will be more people who need therapy for injuries, surgeries, and other conditions that come with aging, such as arthritis and heart problems. Also, today's population of older Americans is much more active than people of the same age twenty or thirty years ago. As older people engage in more strenuous activities, such as sports, they will have injuries and conditions that require treatment. As the percentage of Americans that are seniors increases, so will the need for therapists.

Career Stepping-Stones

Is a career as a physical or occupational therapy assistant a bridge to becoming an actual therapist? The answer is yes and no. Working as an assistant may help people decide if a career in physical or occupational therapy is right for them. It is a hands-on immersion in the field, showing them what a therapy career is really like. Since becoming an assistant requires only two years of higher education, it is more attainable than a therapist career, which often requires a master's degree or even a doctorate. However, the two-year program for certification as a physical or occupational therapy assistant is not something that can be built upon if the assistant decides to pursue a full-blown therapist career. Generally, one will have to start again as a student and spend all of the time required to obtain the necessary degrees. Assistant certification courses will not usually shorten this time period. Therefore, if a student is interested in becoming a therapist, it is best to start a college career with that goal in mind, rather than working as an assistant and then going back to school to start a new program.

Working as a physical or occupational therapy aide is a good stepping-stone to becoming an assistant, however. It provides immersion in the field before the student pursues the necessary higher education to be a therapy assistant or a therapist, and in most cases it requires only a high school diploma.

Chapter 2

Physical Therapy Assistant

A physical therapy aide is largely tasked with doing support jobs, such as setting up and cleaning treatment areas. An aide's contact with patients is usually limited to greeting them from the other side of a desk while helping with paperwork, or perhaps helping a patient from a waiting area to a treatment area. A physical therapy assistant, on the other hand, is more active in treating patients and relates to them on a more personal level.

A physical therapy assistant performs tasks that are administrative, such as keeping accurate patient records, and supportive, such as setting up equipment for the treatments that will be performed that day. An assistant also supports patients by helping them move from one area to another or applying heat or massage therapies. In some cases, the assistant plays an important role in treatment, helping patients perform exercises and use equipment. Depending on the facility where he or she works, state regulations, and the role of the supervising physical therapist, an assistant might even administer a patient's entire treatment on a regular basis.

Location, Location, Location

In the field of physical therapy, there are many different settings where one can work. The most common place to practice physical therapy is in a hospital setting. While some hospitals have an all-purpose physical and occupational therapy department, a physical therapy assistant can often specialize within the hospital setting. Common areas of focus include acute care, pediatric care, orthopedic care, and geriatric care.

Acute care is physical therapy for patients who have been admitted to the hospital for short-term care because of illness or injury. The goal is to get the patient quickly to the point at which he or she can be discharged.

Pediatric care involves treating children for physical problems resulting from injuries, disorders, or diseases. It also involves early detection of health problems. Physical therapy assistants work with children who need help with fine motor skills,

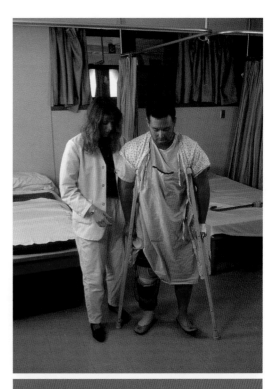

In acute care settings in hospitals, patients receive physical therapy to speed their recovery from injuries or surgery.

balance, or processing sensory information. They also work with children who have disorders such as cerebral palsy or spina bifida and need help with movement.

Orthopedic care includes diagnosing, managing, and treating disorders and injuries related to the musculoskeletal system. These injuries and conditions may result from sports injuries, arthritis, amputations, and other orthopedic

Equipment such as arm bicycles can help elderly patients regain mobility and strength in their limbs.

surgeries. Orthopedic care also involves the treatment of diseases affecting the muscles, joints, bones, or ligaments of the body. This type of physical therapy often takes place in an outpatient setting.

Geriatric care focuses on people who are going through the aging process. These physical therapy assistants help elderly people who have lost function and mobility due to arthritis, osteoporosis, cancer, Alzheimer's disease, balance problems, hip or joint replacement, or other conditions. Typical goals are to reduce pain and increase fitness and mobility.

Other Types of PT

Some physical therapy assistants work with people who need rehabilitation after experiencing cardiovascular and pulmonary problems. This therapy tends to focus on regaining endurance and independence. Another type is neurological physical therapy, or treatment of issues related to spinal cord injuries, multiple sclerosis, Parkinson's disease, stroke, and other diseases and disorder of the nervous system. Often patients must cope with vision loss, balance issues, or paralysis, and therapy helps them regain some everyday independence.

Physical therapy also takes place in rehabilitation hospitals, where some patients are sent after being treated in a regular hospital. These patients require an extended period of recovery and rehabilitation in a setting specially focused on those goals. Here, a physical therapy assistant usually works on a team with other therapists, such as occupational, speech, and recreational therapists and assistants.

Working in a hospital setting as a physical therapy assistant often pays a lower hourly wage, but there is greater predictability and job security than in some other settings. An assistant in a clinic setting may be sent home without pay if there aren't enough patients on the schedule on a given day, whereas a job in a hospital usually guarantees forty hours a week.

Beyond Hospitals

Instead of working in a hospital setting, a physical therapy assistant might work in an outpatient clinic not directly connected to a specific hospital. These clinics may be independently owned or part of a national chain. Many of them specialize in helping people who have suffered from sports injuries.

Many school districts employ physical therapists and assistants. They usually work with children who have disabilities and are enrolled in a special education program. Physical therapy is often part of their specific IEP, or individualized education program,

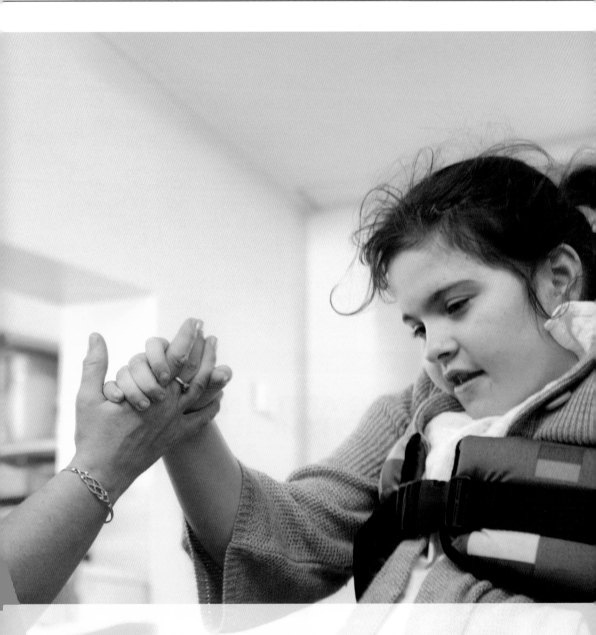

Disabled students may receive physical therapy in a school setting.

which is the plan for that child's education developed by educators, specialists, and parents. The advantage to working as a physical therapy assistant in a school setting is that the assistant will usually have summers off when school is not in session.

A growing area of physical therapy is home care, in which a therapist and assistant travel to a patient's home and perform treatments there. This is done for patients who are unable to leave their homes and travel to a therapy facility.

Finally, physical therapists and assistants may work in settings such as doctors' offices, nursing homes, universities, and adult day care facilities.

LOOKING AT THE NUMBERS: PHYSICAL THERAPY ASSISTANTS

It is a good time to be a physical therapy assistant. According to the U.S. government's employment outlook statistics, the number of physical therapy assistants is expected to grow by 46 percent between 2010 and 2020. This is a much faster rate than in most occupations. Demand for physical therapy is expected to increase because of the health care needs of a growing elderly population.

A Day in the Life

What exactly does a physical therapy assistant do during a normal workday? He or she is typically involved in patient treatment.

Treatment usually begins after a doctor's referral and patient evaluation, in which the physical therapist and the assistant work together to examine the patient and develop a plan for him or her. The evaluation starts with basic findings by the therapist, such as the age and gender of the patient, the location and intensity of the pain, and the patient's history. The history includes details such as whether an accident or injury created the patient's pain, if he or she has received treatment or previous therapy for the condition, and whether he or she is currently using any medications for pain. The evaluation also describes what the therapist finds in physically examining the patient, such as a limited range of motion or pain.

Finally, the document lists a specific treatment plan for the patient. Details typically include how frequently and for how long the patient should attend physical therapy, what kinds of exercises the patient will do, and what modalities (treatment tools) will be used. The treatment plan states what the specific goals are for the patient, such as returning to a normal range of motion or decreasing pain.

Once the treatment plan is established, the physical therapy assistant often assists in or actually conducts the treatment sessions. The assistant may use one or several types of equipment in the treatment. Besides modalities such as electric stimulation, ultrasound, or massage, the plan might include machinery such as a treadmill,

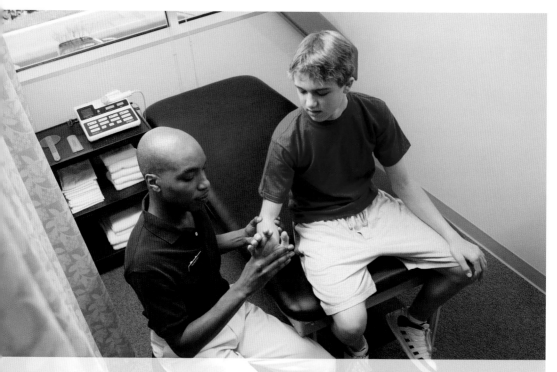

The supervising physical therapist examines a boy's hand and fingers to evaluate his condition and create a treatment plan. The assistant will help carry out the plan.

elliptical machine, or pedal exerciser, which is similar to a stationary bicycle. Assistants also help patients with traction, which pulls on joints and stretches them to relieve back or neck pain. These treatment approaches are intended to help the patient regain muscle tone and reverse the effects of atrophy. Atrophy is a condition in which the muscle is weakened and decreases in size from lack of use.

Physical Therapy Equipment

Physical therapy assistants may use other types of equipment with patients as well. Commonly used tools include resistance exercise bands, which are like large, flat rubber bands. These come in eight levels of resistance or strength; each level comes in a different color. Resistance bands are used in several different ways. The physical therapy assistant may hold one end while the patient pulls on the other. Or the patient may use the band by himself or herself by stepping on one end or looping it over a doorknob or railing. The band provides resistance and strengthens muscles. Weights, such as those that only weigh a few pounds, are also used to help with resistance and building muscle tone.

Patients may use large exercise balls, which look like giant beach balls with nonslip surfaces. They can sit on the ball to improve their balance and coordination, or they can do sit-ups and other exercises with it. Exercise balls come in several sizes, depending on the patient's height, and they can usually hold up to 600 pounds (272 kg).

Finally, a physical therapy assistant may help a patient through the use of a Nintendo Wii or a similar interactive video gaming system. This is becoming more popular in physical therapy. Moving along with the game and swinging the remote—such as in Wii bowling or golf—helps the patient with balance and coordination. The Nintendo Wii also has the advantage of instantly providing feedback, such as an assessment of balance, to the therapist.

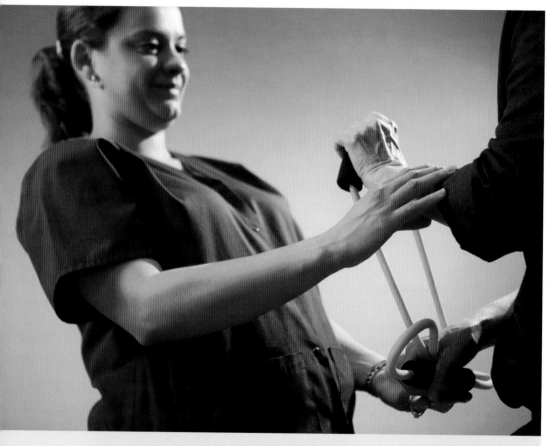

A physical therapy assistant teaches a patient to use an exercise band. The band provides resistance and helps strengthen muscles.

Aside from helping conduct treatment, the assistant will often observe and record the patient's progress during a particular session and help assess his or her overall response to treatment. Depending on the size and type of the therapy facility, the assistant may also do clerical tasks, such as filling out billing or insurance forms or ordering supplies.

Hours and Days

A physical therapy assistant's hours depend on the type of facility that employs him or her. In a hospital setting, assistants may have a set schedule of Monday through Friday during normal working hours of about 8 AM to 5 PM. In an independent clinic, however, hours might include evenings and weekends to accommodate patient schedules more easily. This can be a way to attract customers to the facility. Therapy assistants who travel to patients' homes must structure their days around those appointments, which may occur during nonstandard working hours. Their schedules are also more likely to vary from week to week. Physical therapy assistants usually work a forty-hour week, although they can choose to work part-time.

Being a physical therapy assistant is a career that can be very flexible or very structured, depending on the facility where the assistant works and the scope of tasks that he or she is given to do. An assistant whose work is largely clerical or who just supports a physical therapist will have less flexibility than an assistant who does actual hands-on therapy. The career can be adapted to the preferences of individual assistants, such as their desire to work a fixed schedule or have a more fluid arrangement.

Chapter 3

Getting Started in PT

So what does it take to be a physical therapy assistant? Unlike becoming a physical therapist, which may require five to seven years of higher education and often a master's degree or a doctorate, a career as a physical therapy assistant is attainable with only two years of college-level courses.

Education

A physical therapy assistant education results in an associate of science (AS) degree from a college or university that is accredited by the Commission on Accreditation in Physical Therapy Education (CAPTE). The program prepares students to begin work as a physical therapy assistant (PTA) as soon as they graduate. Accreditation ensures that a college's PTA program provides students with the skills needed for the job. It ensures that the teachers at the school are qualified and that the course requirements and information taught are current. It also means that graduates of the program have proven that they have gained the knowledge needed to work successfully in the field. Schools that offer two-year PTA degrees are often community colleges, but many regular colleges and universities offer the program as well.

Students must meet certain requirements for admission to a PTA program. Candidates usually need a grade point average of 2.8 or higher in high school (or in college, if they have already taken college-level classes). They must pass assessment tests in reading and language, and there are often class requirements in math and medical terminology. Some schools require prospective PTA students to complete a certain number of hours observing a physical therapy assistant at work. They may also have to pass health and drug screenings and a criminal background check before they can participate in clinical internships.

From Acceptance to Enrollment

In most colleges, applicants who meet the admission requirements are enrolled in the PTA program on a first-come, first-served basis. Typically, one's program can be started in the fall semester only. Students are usually required to complete a certain number of credit hours in general education, including science and social science courses, as well as courses specific to becoming a physical therapy assistant. PTA courses include anatomy, psychology, therapeutic practices, exercise techniques, pathology, orthopedics, rehabilitation of neurological conditions, and physics. Students

Required courses for physical therapy assistant degrees include anatomy, the study of the body's structure.

are also expected to learn cardiopulmonary resuscitation (CPR) and basic first aid.

Students must complete two clinical internships in which they learn about physical therapy under the close supervision of a physical therapist and physical therapy assistants. The internships must take place at a clinic, hospital, or other certified facility. These experiences ensure that students understand the responsibilities and tasks involved in being a PTA.

Skills and Abilities

Besides college-level education in a PTA program, students need certain skills and personal qualities if they expect to be successful in this field.

Compassion is one of the most important qualities. Physical therapy is a profession entirely devoted to helping people heal from illnesses, accidents, and injuries. Successful PTAs should have compassion for patients, showing empathy for what they go through, and should enjoy helping them feel better. Because PTAs spend most of their time interacting with patients, they need to be personable, courteous, and friendly. A patient may have difficulty working with a PTA who is not friendly and encouraging. This could impede the patient's progress, no matter how good the physical therapy exercises and modalities might be.

Potential PTAs should be detail-oriented, with good organizational skills and the ability to notice details, especially when observing patients. They also need the ability to keep accurate records, write clearly and understandably, and follow written directions exactly to make sure patients receive high-quality care. Clear communication among the physical therapist, physical therapy assistant, clerical staff, and doctors is essential.

Physical therapy assistants need to be healthy and have physical stamina. They spend a large part of the day on their feet and do a lot of moving as they work with patients. They may be standing, kneeling, stooping, or bending for long periods of time, as well as lifting and supporting less mobile patients. Someone who is not physically healthy and able to move freely won't be able to do everything necessary to help patients.

PTAs also need to have manual dexterity, which means they should be comfortable using their hands for effective massages, manual therapy, and other therapeutic exercises. They should be comfortable setting up equipment and treatment areas.

Listening and Observing

Potential PTAs need to have excellent communication skills, both verbal and nonverbal. In particular, they need to be good listeners, especially when interacting with the supervising physical therapist and with patients.

According to Olga Dreeben-Irimia, author of *Introduction to Physical Therapy for Physical Therapist Assistants*, there are several different types of listening that are relevant to a physical therapy assistant. Some of these include:

- **Analytical listening.** An example is listening to a patient to gain information from his or her description of pain.

A physical therapy assistant reviews exercises with a patient during a therapy session. When communicating with patients, listening attentively can be as important as talking.

- **Directed listening.** This means listening to a patient's answers to specific questions, such as what activities increase or decrease pain.
- **Attentive listening.** This includes listening to the physical therapist give specific recommendations for a patient's treatment.
- **Courteous listening.** In this type of listening, the assistant might listen to a patient telling a story or talking about subjects unrelated to treatment.

Nonverbal communication includes paying attention to facial expressions, eye contact, and body language in patients. It can also include paying attention to a patient's personal appearance and grooming habits, which might indicate something about the person's ability to take care of himself or herself. Knowledge of body language can help the PTA understand if a patient seems open to communicating and being helped or seems withdrawn and unlikely to participate fully in treatment.

Testing and Licensing

Once students complete the two-year physical therapy assistant program and earn an associate's degree, they need to become licensed before getting a job. While regulations differ from state to state, most states require this licensing. Students must pass the National Physical Therapy Examination (NPTE), which assesses candidates' basic entry-level competence. This helps protect the public by making sure that people entering the physical therapy profession are qualified to provide care. The exam is

LISTEN UP!

Effective listening is a primary tool for interacting with patients, building trust, and gaining the patient's cooperation for treatment. What are some examples of effective listening for physical therapy assistants?

- They focus their attention on the patient.
- They use smiling and eye contact to encourage the patient to speak.
- They pay attention to the patient's nonverbal communication.
- They ask the patient for clarification when necessary.
- They repeat what the patient says to show that they understand it.
- They take notes as necessary to remember important details.
- They use their own body language to encourage the patient or show understanding.
- They do not interrupt the patient.
- They show that they empathize with the patient.

Because listening is so important in this field, those who plan to become physical therapy assistants should take time to learn and practice effective listening skills.

taken on a computer and is offered in specific testing locations in every state in the country. It consists of four sections, each with fifty questions. Scores range from two hundred to eight hundred points, but the minimum passing score is six hundred points. The Federation of State Boards of Physical Therapy (FSBPT) conducts the exam.

In addition, each state has its own board or department that regulates physical therapy workers, and states may require additional exams before granting candidates a license to work in this field. Licenses may be valid for only a certain period of time, such as two years, before they must be renewed. Physical therapy assistants with licensure may be required to take continuing education courses to renew their license.

Some students who earn physical therapy assistant degrees and licensing go on to take

Students must pass the National Physical Therapy Examination for PTAs, which is taken on a computer, in order to become licensed as a physical therapy assistant.

higher education courses to qualify for jobs in health care administration, management, or education. Others simply continue to work as PTAs for the duration of their careers. A few may choose to go back to school to qualify as physical therapists. However, the coursework involved in becoming a PT requires many more years of education, and PTA courses normally do not count toward the prerequisites. It is possible to pursue a physical therapy degree by taking night and weekend courses while still working as a PTA, but it will take even longer to achieve.

Chapter 4

Occupational Therapy Assistant

U nlike physical therapy, which focuses on alleviating pain and helping patients regain use of an injured body part, occupational therapy is more concerned with helping patients cope with their condition. In occupational therapy, patients develop new skills for everyday tasks in order to live as independently as possible.

As in physical therapy, in occupational therapy many of the basic tasks are assigned to occupational therapy aides. They may be responsible for cleaning treatment areas between patients and at the end of the day, helping patients to the treatment area and back again, and doing paperwork and other clerical tasks.

The occupational therapy assistant (OTA) is usually more involved in patient treatment, depending on the size of the facility where he or she works. In a small facility, the occupational therapy assistant may perform administrative tasks, such as recording observations in the patient's record and handling billing and telephone calls. OTAs may also do setup and cleanup tasks, especially making sure any equipment needed for a patient's treatment is ready in the treatment area. Occupational therapy often involves a lot of tools and equipment, and it is important to make maximum use of the time scheduled for a patient's treatment.

Types of Occupational Therapy

Occupational therapy is a form of rehabilitation that helps people achieve greater independence in caring for themselves and performing everyday tasks. The American Occupational Therapy Association (AOTA) lists a number of different types of occupational therapy on its Web site, http://www.aota.org. The categories are based on the population served, the type of diagnosis, and the kind of setting. For example, some occupational therapists work exclusively with children and youth, usually in schools, clinics, or homes. Some work with people who suffer from mental illness, while others work with the elderly to help them with productive aging. Many occupational therapists work in the rehabilitation field. Some focus on workplace and industrial rehabilitation, working with people who are trying to resume their jobs after an illness or injury. In some facilities, occupational therapists and their assistants may work with people in all of these categories.

An occupational therapy assistant works with the supervising occupational therapist to evaluate patients and develop treatment plans for them. The treatment plan begins with a diagnosis of the patient's condition or injury. The occupational therapist and OTA evaluate

The Web site of the American Occupational Therapy Association, http://www.aota.org, provides a wealth of information about the different types of occupational therapy.

the patient's range of motion in the parts of the body affected by the injury or condition, as well as the level of pain the patient is experiencing. Then they evaluate the patient's limitations in areas of daily living, including movement (walking, lifting, carrying), self-care (bathing, dressing, eating, toileting), home management (household chores, shopping, driving, taking care of a family), and work and community activities.

Making a Plan

After the occupational therapist and the assistant complete the evaluation, they create a treatment plan to use with the patient. It includes the expected number of visits and the period of time the treatment is expected to last, as well as specific activities to focus on. The therapy activities must meet the patient's needs and capabilities and be tailored to the activities in his or her life.

Once the treatment plan is created, the occupational therapy assistant helps the supervising therapist carry out the treatment. Again, the OTA's level of involvement depends on the policies of the facility and the requirements of the state where he or she works. The assistant may carry out a large portion of the treatment or just certain parts of it. In some cases, the OTA may simply be present, observing and helping, while the therapist does the treatment.

The OTA may help a patient with stretching activities to limber up muscles before more strenuous treatment activities. An OTA may teach a patient the correct way to move from a bed to a wheelchair, or ways to compensate for lost motor skills when he or she returns to the workplace. In occupational therapy with children, treatment might consist of playing games intended to help with coordination, perhaps using large balls or trampolines. For children with emotional difficulties, the OTA can use a large weighted doll or teddy bear to make the child feel comforted. Toys are often used in occupational therapy with children to capture their interest and make therapy easier and more fun. For children with developmental disabilities, the OTA may teach everyday

An OTA uses a large ball to help a disabled child stretch and move.

skills to help them become more independent.

Occupational therapy treatment usually includes services such as teaching a patient new ways to approach a task that he or she can no longer do, how to break an activity down into small achievable tasks, and how to adapt an environment to make it easier for the disabled person to function. Treatment might also use creative therapies, such as art or crafts, to benefit the patient's mental state or motor skills.

Tools of the Trade

Occupational therapy uses many different types of tools. Braces and slings may be used to support a body part or isolate an injury so that the patient can learn to compensate with another body part or muscle group. Some patients may wear gait belts or transfer belts, wide belts that allow the

CREATING THE TOOLS

One interesting job that directly supports the work of occupational therapists and their assistants is that of a rehabilitation engineer. These professionals are specially trained to adapt existing products or design new ones to meet the specific needs of people with disabilities. They may adapt computers or typewriters for people with limited hand dexterity, or put handles on familiar kitchen utensils to make them easier to grip. If an occupational therapist feels that a patient needs a piece of equipment that isn't currently available, he or she can ask a rehabilitation engineer to design something to meet that need.

therapist to hold on to them when they are walking or moving. These tools lessen the risk of falls with unsteady patients. The therapy assistant can grab the belt and use it to support a patient or safely lower a patient into a chair or onto the ground. For patients who have lost much of their ability to use their hands, the OTA may help them learn to use a head pointer, mouth stick, or optical pointer to command a computer, do word processing, or use other forms of communication. The may also teach such patients to use everyday implements, such as eating utensils and pencils, with modifications that make them easier for people with disabilities to use.

An occupational therapy assistant may help improve the quality of life of people with debilitating or terminal illnesses, helping them deal with fatigue and stress and learn to accomplish tasks that might become increasingly difficult. The OTA may help someone who has had an amputation learn how to put on a prosthetic limb. In addition, an OTA may educate families about how to care for a family member who has suffered a disabling illness or injury, such as how to modify their home or how to use special adaptive equipment.

Cheering Them On

In addition to performing some treatment tasks, an occupational therapy assistant may have an even more important role as a kind of cheerleader for patients. The OTA often supports and encourages patients during treatment, helping them maintain a positive outlook and focus on good outcomes. Therefore, projecting a cheerful, optimistic attitude is vital. The OTA must also communicate well with other members of the treatment team—including the supervising occupational therapist, the patient's doctor, and families—so that everyone works together for the patient's benefit.

The assistant typically observes and records each treatment session, especially noting the patient's progress, attitude, and behavior during the treatment. This is important because many occupational therapy patients are facing permanent changes in their lifestyles and their motivation and attitudes may be low due to discouragement.

Settings and Roles

Occupational therapy takes place in a variety of settings. The role of the assistant varies depending on the setting where the therapy is taking place. Therapy can be conducted in a hospital, and many hospitals even have simulated everyday settings such as kitchens, stores, automobiles, restaurants, and streets to help patients practice everyday skills.

Many hospitals and rehabilitation facilities have everyday settings such as kitchens to help patients practice daily skills.

Occupational therapy also occurs in outpatient clinics that are not specifically connected to a hospital. Patients receive OT in residential facilities such as group homes, long-term residential facilities, rehabilitation hospitals, nursing homes, and adult day care facilities. Some occupational therapy takes place in patients' homes, especially if the patient cannot travel to a clinic or hospital. Occupational therapists may work in a school setting, particularly with disabled special education students, to make sure that their learning environment is adapted to their needs. Finally, some occupational therapists choose to be traveling therapists, moving from one facility to another, depending on the needs of a facility at a particular time. They may work at a facility for as little as eight weeks or as long as nine months.

The variety of settings where an occupational therapy assistant can work makes it a career that can be adapted to the assistant. OTAs may work full-time or part-time. In a hospital or residential facility setting, they may work a set schedule and regular hours. An assistant who works with patients in their homes or as a traveling OTA may have a more flexible schedule. Occupational therapy assistants in a clinic setting may have to work nights and weekends to meet the needs of their clients. Assistants in a school setting will have vacations and summers off.

Chapter 5

Getting Started in OT

J ust as with a physical therapy assistant, becoming an occupational therapy assistant is a career goal that can be reached with just two years of higher education. Occupational therapy assistant education usually results in an associate of applied science (AAS) degree. This credential is easier to achieve than those for occupational therapy, which now requires at least a master's degree and often a doctoral degree.

The best place to start training as an OTA is in high school. Courses in biology and health science can help a student earn admission to a college OTA program. Doing volunteer work in a health care setting, such as a nursing home or occupational therapist's office, can also be helpful.

Higher Education

There are more than three hundred schools with occupational therapy assistant programs. Some are community colleges; others are regular four-year colleges and universities. When choosing a school that offers a two-year

OTA program, it is important to find one that is accredited through the Accreditation Council for Occupational Therapy Education (ACOTE). This accreditation is given only to schools that have demonstrated that they provide the academic classes and fieldwork necessary for an entry-level position as an OTA. Schools must show that they educate students according to the latest knowledge and practices in the field of occupational therapy and that they give students a strong understanding of the roles and responsibilities of an OTA. Graduating students must

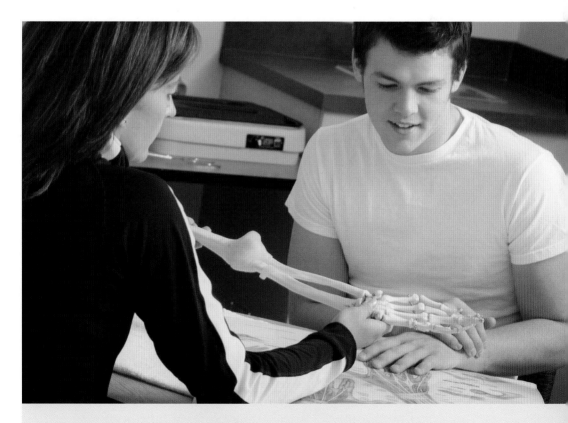

Students hoping to become OTAs must study anatomy and physiology as part of their education.

also understand the ethics and values of the profession of occupational therapy.

Most colleges have separate requirements for students to be admitted into the OTA program, apart from the general requirements necessary to be enrolled in the college overall. These might include a certain grade point average and completion of introductory courses in biology or anatomy. Students can't be convicted felons, as this will prevent them from becoming employed as OTAs, so they may be required to go through a criminal background check. They also need to have medical insurance, a health examination, a drug screening, vaccination against diseases like hepatitis B, and certification in CPR. All of these factors will affect whether students are admitted to the program.

Programs, which begin once a year in the fall, are often highly competitive, admitting only a limited number of students. Those students are admitted based on how many requirements they have met, their grades, and their other activities. Potential students also need to be strong, since they will have to support and lift patients, and physically fit enough for the long periods of moving and standing that go with the job.

Hitting the Books—and More

Once accepted into an OTA program, students take a wide variety of courses. These typically include anatomy and physiology (human structure and function), principles of occupational therapy, psychology, medical terminology, mathematics, therapeutic activities and interventions, mental health, computers, and electives in speech, fine arts, and humanities. Usually, the general introductory

A young patient with cerebral palsy receives occupational therapy in a home setting. OTAs learn how to use therapeutic interventions during their clinical fieldwork.

courses are taken during the first year, and courses dealing with occupational therapy techniques and practices are taken during the second year.

The program includes two clinical fieldwork experiences totaling two semesters. One is a practicum supervised by

LOOKING AT THE NUMBERS: OCCUPATIONAL THERAPY ASSISTANTS

According to the U.S. Department of Labor, it's a good time to begin a career as an occupational therapy assistant. Between 2010 and 2020, jobs in occupational therapy are expected to grow by 41 percent, which is much faster than the 14-percent average for all other jobs. The government projects that nearly seventeen thousand new occupational therapy assistant jobs will be created by 2020. In 2010, thirty-six thousand people were employed as OTAs.

an instructor, and the other is a semester of full-time work that is supervised by a licensed occupational therapist. These experiences help students apply their OTA skills in a real-life setting with real patients. They also help students understand the demands and responsibilities that go with the job. The first semester of fieldwork is called Level 1. It focuses on promoting the student's ability to communicate with clients and develop a basic understanding of clients' needs. This fieldwork is completed while the student is also taking academic classes. The second fieldwork experience, known as Level 2, is meant to bridge the gap between academic studies and entry-level employment as an OTA. It is done after all academic work is completed, and it generally takes sixteen weeks of full-time work.

Because of the necessity of real-world clinical experience, there are currently no OTA programs that are offered completely online. Some programs may offer certain courses in an online format, but much of what a student needs to learn for a successful OTA career requires hands-on, in-person education.

Key Professional and Personal Qualities

In programs for OTA education, there are a number of areas that the American Occupational Therapy Association (AOTA) has determined should be part of the curriculum. These curriculum threads are seen as so important to the OTA profession that they are reinforced throughout the education process. Some of these include:

- Professional behavior, or demonstrating professional attitudes, values, choices, and actions
- Evidence-based practice, or collecting information accurately and using data to help patients
- Awareness of cultural diversity, or appreciating and understanding the different ideas and cultures encountered in a typical occupational therapy practice
- Collaboration within a team, or appreciating the value of teamwork and cooperating with other therapists and colleagues to treat patients
- Lifelong learning, or continuing to learn and grow in the profession throughout one's working career

Occupational therapy can involve relearning simple tasks such as lacing and tying. OTAs must be able to support their patients in times of frustration.

In addition to education and practice in these areas, there are personal qualities that are needed to become a successful OTA. OTAs should be detail-oriented, since they need to follow written and oral directions from the supervising occupational therapist carefully. They may also be responsible for maintaining a patient's written medical records, including transcribing notes about treatment sessions. Since so much of their time is spent interacting with patients, they need to have strong interpersonal skills. They need to be friendly and courteous, as well as good, clear communicators. They should be compassionate, as they will often be working with patients who are struggling to accomplish the basic activities of life and who may be discouraged or even angry about their situation. In short, OTAs need to be caring and encouraging in order to work successfully with diverse individuals and to ensure that patients have a positive occupational therapy experience.

Testing and Licensing

Once students have completed their coursework and clinical experience and have received their two-year degree, in most states they will need to become licensed before they can begin working. This may require passing an exam to show that they have the necessary knowledge and skills. OTAs can also choose to take the Certified Occupational Therapy Assistant (COTA) exam offered by the National Board for Certification in Occupational Therapy (NBCOT). If they pass this exam, they are officially certified by NBCOT. Many employers require this certification before they will employ an OTA.

Once OTAs are working, most states will require them to take continuing education courses to maintain their license. Ways to do this may include taking additional coursework at a college or technical school, attending workshops, and participating in professional seminars. OTAs can also continue learning by visiting the Web sites of state governments and occupational therapy organizations, where there may be event calendars, professional discussion forums, and news and articles related to the profession. Some employers offer mentorship programs, in which OTAs can work with an experienced occupational therapist to continue to develop their professional abilities.

With enough experience and professional development, OTAs may be able to obtain supervisory positions within their field. These might include managing an occupational therapy practice, teaching in an OTA program, or doing research in the occupational therapy field.

A person who has completed a two-year degree in occupational therapy can choose to go back to school and earn additional degrees to become an occupational therapist. Because this is a job that requires at least a master's degree and often a doctorate, it may be challenging to complete the necessary education while working full-time. However, since becoming an occupational therapist requires so much time and money, becoming an OTA first may be a good way to see if working in the occupational therapy field is what a student wants to do before pursuing the extra education to become an occupational therapist.

Chapter 6

Launching a Career

O nce two years of education have been completed, and students have earned their associate's degree and passed their licensing exam, it's time to find—and keep—a job in the physical or occupational therapy field. Fortunately, both areas are growing at a much faster rate than other types of careers, and this generally means that there are many openings for PTAs and OTAs.

Entering the Field

Candidates for PTA and OTA jobs need to remember that there are many different settings where these jobs may be available. There are traditional hospital settings, perhaps in a rehabilitation department or in surgical or other hospital wards. Nursing homes and residential facilities for the elderly are also good places to look for jobs. Job seekers can look into private physical therapy clinics and home health care companies as well. It largely depends on the type of setting and schedule that a job seeker is looking for. A hospital setting will provide regular hours, usually

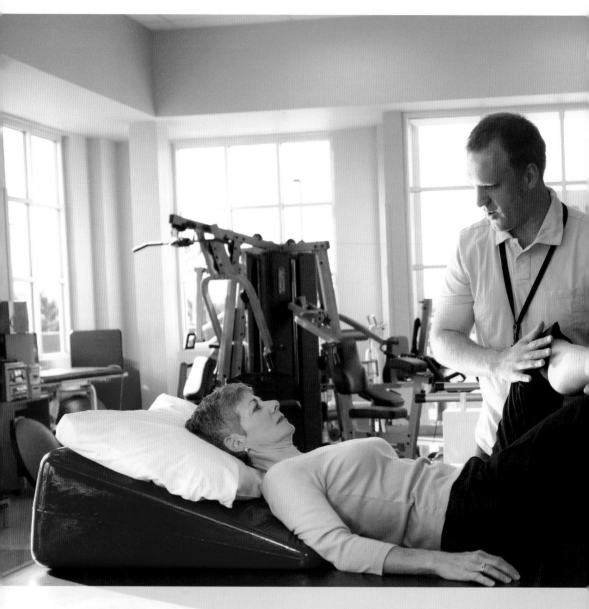

A therapist works with a patient on a therapy bed in a physical therapy clinic.

Monday through Friday, while a private clinic or home health care company might require evening and weekend hours. Job applicants can usually choose whether they want to work full-time or part-time, no matter what the setting.

Even though both PTA and OTA training require practical fieldwork, an assistant's first real job in therapy is often his or her first taste of what it's really like to work in the health care field. It can be the gateway to future positions in health care, either by advancing into a managerial position or by going back to school to become a therapist or other professional. The first job is also the first time that most assistants are actively involved with patients—and other health care professionals such as doctors, administrators, and therapists—on a recurring basis.

Since they are now part of a health care team for the

long term, new assistants will find that the relationships they encounter in the workplace will be a little different than they were during fieldwork. They will probably be given greater responsibilities, such as record keeping and paperwork. They will also see their relationships with therapy patients develop over a longer period of time. This can be a challenge, since they are likely to see more of the ups and downs that patients experience over the course of treatment.

They may also find that patients and health care professionals treat them differently now that they are permanent, paid staff members. Patients and professionals who might take it easy on a student will no longer do so with a real staff member. New assistants must be willing to accept constructive criticism. They must also understand that people who have tried to display a good attitude in front of a student may not do so with an actual therapy assistant.

The Dos and Don'ts

Because a physical or occupational therapy assistant is now part of a health care team, there are things to remember in the workplace. First of all, if there is a dress code, the assistant needs to follow it. Some therapy facilities require staff members to dress in the same kind of scrubs that doctors and nurses wear, both for ease of movement and to help show that they are professionals. However, other therapy facilities may allow staff to dress in casual street clothes. In that case, it is important to wear clothing that allows for freedom of movement, since therapy assistants often do a great deal of bending,

Performing therapy with a patient requires clothing that is appropriate and does not restrict movement.

lifting, stretching, and moving. Clothing that is constricting or inappropriate (such as low-cut shirts or high heels for a female) will make it difficult for the assistant to do his or her job and maintain professionalism. A newly hired assistant should ask specifically about the facility's dress code—and then follow it exactly.

As a member of a health care team, it is essential to maintain good communication and follow directions carefully. When therapy assistants carry out the treatment plan established by the supervising therapist, they must be sure to do exactly what is prescribed for the patient's treatment activities, especially in the beginning. They must follow each procedure exactly, whether it involves using particular pieces of equipment or filling out paperwork for billing. Procedures are established for health and safety reasons, as well as for making processes like billing and record keeping uniform and complete. Following procedures in a sloppy or incomplete fashion will only frustrate other team members.

It is also vital that assistants take direction well. If they get defensive about having mistakes pointed out, or they fail to do what they are told to do with a certain patient, it only makes things more difficult for everyone on the team.

Attitude Is Everything

Displaying a good attitude toward patients is very important, especially now that an assistant may see the same people for a period of many months. Patients are not always cooperative and pleasant in a therapy setting. They may be surly or resistant to treatment, simply because they are in pain, are frustrated about their physical limitations, or are angry about having to do therapy. A patient may be in therapy for the first time after a lifetime of good health and might resent the sudden limitations on his or her daily activities.

Assistants must be pleasant no matter how patients act and must not allow themselves to show anger or irritation. They should remain professional and be patient with people who are experiencing physical ailments and finding themselves unable to function normally. They must be willing to listen, even if a patient wants to tell a story about

A VOICE FROM THE FIELD

What is it really like to work as a physical therapy assistant? Todd Bedward has worked as an assistant in the physical therapy field for more than a decade. He works with people who have balance problems stemming from inner ear disturbances, knee or hip injuries, and brain injuries. He also helps treat people with Parkinson's, Alzheimer's, and Lou Gehrig's disease.

He told the All Allied Health Schools Web site, "Physical therapists are a fun group of people to work with. There isn't a lot of stress, as there is in the business world. You are what you are. You try to do the best you can." When asked what he liked most about his job, he said that he enjoyed being able to help patients by figuring out the puzzle of what's wrong with them and how to fix it. "I love the fact that when we're done with them, they're fine. They're back to their lives."

something unrelated to therapy. When listening to patients discuss their condition, they should say things that are positive and encouraging, rather than just commiserating.

Therapy assistants may need to come to terms with the loss of a patient, especially if they work in a nursing home or home health care setting. They need to understand the fact that some people come to therapy toward the end of their lives and accept that as part of the job. Most hospitals have counselors who can help staff members in especially difficult situations, such as the death of a young patient or a patient that the assistant thought was progressing well. If the loss of a patient is affecting an assistant's attitude or ability to perform the job well, he or she needs to seek help to come to terms with that loss.

Lifelong Learning and Networking

As assistants become part of a therapy team and become accustomed to the job, they may find opportunities for further education. Depending on the state where they work, they may be required to take continuing education courses to maintain their license. In some cases, an employer will help pay for this additional training or even cover the cost entirely. Assistants should also take advantage of any on-the-job training their employer offers.

There are organizations dedicated to the professional growth of people who work in the physical or occupational therapy fields. These organizations provide current news about the profession, networking opportunities with other therapists and assistants, and information about upcoming trainings and continuing education. For physical therapists, there is the American Physical Therapy Association (APTA), at http://www.apta.org, and for occupational therapists, the American Occupational Therapy Association (AOTA), at http://www.aota.org. Both organizations' Web sites offer information about jobs, career management, and therapy practices, as well as resources for students. There are also links to helpful podcasts and videos, social media, and blogs in which therapists share knowledge and answer each other's questions. There are sections of the Web sites specifically for therapy assistants.

Physical and occupational therapy assistants are likely to find that the field of therapy is growing. They should be able to develop a career that pays well with only two years of higher education. There should be job security due to the fact that there will be a steadily increasing

Being a therapy assistant can be a very rewarding career for those who like to help others heal and regain a normal, healthy life.

number of patients in the years to come. The United States has a large population of baby boomers who are entering the part of their lives in which they may need therapy, either for regular conditions of aging or because of their active lifestyles. Older people are more active than they once were, but this activity, such as exercise and physically taxing hobbies, will likely make them vulnerable to injuries that require therapy to heal. In addition to an aging population, modern medical science has made it likely that more people will survive traumatic injuries, accidents, diseases, and congenital conditions than ever before. This means that more people will need therapy to deal with the results of these conditions. There will also be a large population of military veterans who have suffered injuries in military service and require therapy to help them heal and function in civilian life.

Being a therapy assistant, either in physical or occupational therapy, can be very satisfying. For people who enjoy helping others heal and regain a normal and healthy life, it can be a very rewarding career.

GLOSSARY

acute Requiring or providing short-term medical care.

alleviate To make less severe or more bearable.

arthritis Painful inflammation and stiffness of the joints.

cardiovascular Relating to the heart and blood vessels.

cerebral palsy A condition marked by paralysis and impaired muscle coordination and speech, usually due to an injury to or abnormal development of the brain before birth.

clerical Relating to the work of an office clerk or administrative staff.

commiserate To feel or express sympathy or sorrow.

congenital Existing at or before birth.

dexterity Skill and ease in physical activity, especially in using the hands.

discharge To release a patient from a hospital or course of care.

geriatric Relating to old age or the aging process.

immersion Complete involvement in an activity or interest.

mobility The ability to move freely and easily.

neurological Relating to the nervous system or the branch of medicine that deals with the nervous system.

orthopedics The branch of medicine that deals with the skeletal system and associated structures such as muscles and ligaments.

outpatient A patient who receives medical treatment without being admitted to a hospital.

pediatric Relating to the medical care of children.

prerequisite Something required as a prior condition, such as a course that must be taken before taking a more advanced course.

strenuous Requiring or using great exertion, effort, or energy.

stroke The sudden death of brain cells in a localized area due to inadequate blood flow, often resulting in paralysis, loss of memory and reasoning, and impaired speech.

therapist A person who is skilled in a particular type of therapy.

FOR MORE INFORMATION

American Academy of Physical Therapy (AAPT)
P.O. Box 196
Hazel Crest, IL 60429
(888) 717-AAPT [2278]
Web site: http://www.aaptnet.org
This organization addresses the professional concerns
of the African American physical therapy community.
It promotes new and innovative programs and performs clinical research related to health conditions
found within minority communities. It also encourages minority students to pursue careers in allied
health professions.

American Occupational Therapy Association (AOTA)
4720 Montgomery Lane
Bethesda, MD 20814
(301) 652-2682
Web site: http://www.aota.org
This national professional association represents the
interests and concerns of occupational therapy
practitioners and students of occupational therapy.
Its programs and activities are directed toward
assuring the quality of occupational therapy services, improving consumer access to health care
services, and promoting the professional development of members.

American Physical Therapy Association (APTA)
1111 North Fairfax Street

Alexandria, VA 22314
(703) 684-APTA [2782]
Web site: http://www.apta.org
This membership organization represents physical
therapists, physical therapy assistants, and physical
therapy students. It seeks to improve people's health
and quality of life by advancing physical therapy
practice, education, and research, and by increasing the awareness and understanding of physical
therapy's role in the nation's health care system.

Canadian Association of Occupational Therapists (CAOT)
CTTC Building
3400-1125 Colonel By Drive
Ottawa, ON K1S 5R1
Canada
(800) 434-2268
Web site: http://www.caot.ca
This association provides services, products, events,
and networking opportunities to help occupational
therapists achieve excellence in their professional
practice.

Canadian Physiotherapy Association (CPA)
955 Green Valley Crescent, Suite 270
Ottawa, ON K2C 3V4
Canada
(800) 387-8679
Web site: http://www.physiotherapy.ca
This association represents physiotherapists, physiotherapy
assistants, and physiotherapist students in Canada. Its

members are rehabilitation professionals dedicated to the health, mobility, and fitness of Canadians. The CPA provides resources and education to its members and enables them to learn, share knowledge, and enhance practice.

Web Sites

Due to the changing nature of Internet links, Rosen Publishing has developed an online list of Web sites related to the subject of this book. This site is updated regularly. Please use this link to access the list:

http://www.rosenlinks.com/HCC/Phys

FOR FURTHER READING

Cameron, Michelle H., and Linda G. Monroe. *Physical Rehabilitation for the Physical Therapist Assistant.* St. Louis, MO: Elsevier/Saunders, 2011.

Case-Smith, Jane, and Jane Clifford O'Brien. *Occupational Therapy for Children.* Maryland Heights, MO: Mosby/Elsevier, 2010.

Clynch, Holly M. *The Role of the Physical Therapist Assistant: Regulations and Responsibilities.* Philadelphia, PA: F. A. Davis, 2012.

Dreeben-Irimia, Olga. *Physical Therapy Clinical Handbook for PTAs.* 2nd ed. Burlington, MA: Jones & Bartlett Learning, 2012.

Ferguson Publishing. *Geriatric Care* (Ferguson's Careers in Focus). 3rd ed. New York, NY: Ferguson, 2011.

Flath, Camden. *Therapy Jobs in Educational Settings: Speech, Physical, Occupational & Audiology* (New Careers for the 21st Century: Finding Your Role in the Global Renewal). Broomall, PA: Mason Crest Publishers, 2011.

Harasymiw, Therese. *A Career as a Physical Therapist* (Essential Careers). New York, NY: Rosen Publishing, 2011.

Horn, Geoffrey M. *Sports Therapist* (Cool Careers). Pleasantville, NY: Gareth Stevens, 2009.

Marcil, William Matthew. *Occupational Therapy: What It Is & How It Works.* Clifton Park, NY: Thomson Delmar Learning, 2007.

Moini, Jahangir. *Introduction to Pathology for the Physical Therapist Assistant.* Boston, MA: Jones & Bartlett Learning, 2013.

Pedretti, Lorraine Williams, Heidi McHugh Pendleton, and Winifred Schultz-Krohn. *Pedretti's Occupational Therapy: Practice Skills for Physical Dysfunction.* 7th ed. St. Louis, MO: Elsevier, 2013.

Roy, Serge H., Steven L. Wolf, and David A. Scalzitti. *The Rehabilitation Specialist's Handbook.* 4th ed. Philadelphia, PA: F. A. Davis, 2013.

Theis, Jennifer L. *Clinical Decision Making: Case Studies for the Occupational Therapy Assistant.* Clifton Park, NY: Delmar Cengage Learning, 2011.

Weeks, Zona Roberta. *Opportunities in Occupational Therapy Careers.* Rev. ed. New York, NY: McGraw-Hill, 2007.

Willard, Helen S., and Barbara A. Boyt Schell. *Willard & Spackman's Occupational Therapy.* 12th ed. Philadelphia, PA: Wolters Kluwer Health/Lippincott Williams & Wilkins, 2014.

BIBLIOGRAPHY

AllAlliedHealthSchools.com. "Find Your Physical Therapy Degree Program." 2013. Retrieved December 9, 2012 (http://www.allalliedhealthschools.com/health-careers/physical-therapy/physical-therapy-degree-guide).

AllAlliedHealthSchools.com. "Physical Therapy Assistant Profile." 2013. Retrieved December 9, 2012 (http://www.allalliedhealthschools.com/health-careers/physical-therapy/physical-therapist-assistant-interview).

AllAlliedHealthSchools.com. "Physical Therapy Schools and Careers Resource Center." 2013. Retrieved December 9, 2012 (http://www.allalliedhealthschools.com/health-careers/physical-therapy/physical-therapy-schools-resource-center).

American Occupational Therapy Association. "Occupational Therapy Assistant Model Curriculum." September 30, 2008. Retrieved March 24, 2013 (http://www.aota.org/Educate/EdRes/COE/Other-Education-Documents/OTA-Model-Curriculum.aspx).

American Physical Therapy Association. "Physical Therapist Assistant (PTA) Careers Overview." November 30, 2012. Retrieved December 9, 2012 (http://www.apta.org/PTACareers/Overview).

American Speech-Language-Hearing Association. "Frequently Asked Questions: Speech-Language Pathology Assistants (SLPAs)." 1997–2013. Retrieved January 13, 2013 (http://www.asha.org/certification/faq_slpasst/#d2).

Career Cornerstone Center. "Occupational Therapist Assistant." Retrieved December 9, 2012 (http://

www.careercornerstone.org/alliedhealth/occtherasst/
otasst.htm).

Career Cornerstone Center. "Physical Therapist
Assistant." Retrieved December 9, 2012 (http://
www.careercornerstone.org/alliedhealth/ptasst/
ptasst.htm).

College of Central Florida. "A Day in the Life of a
Physical Therapist Assistant." Retrieved January 16,
2013 (http://www.cf.edu/departments/instruction/
health/pta/life.htm).

Crotti, Nancy. "All in a Day's Work: Physical Therapist
Assistant." StarTribune.com, March 25, 2009.
Retrieved January 16, 2013 (http://www
.startribune.com/jobs/healthcare/32367939
.html?refer=y).

Dreeben-Irimia, Olga. Introduction to Physical Therapy for
Physical Therapist Assistants. Sudbury, MA: Jones and
Bartlett Publishers, 2007.

Education-Portal.com. "Occupational Therapy Assistant
Training Programs and Requirements." 2012.
Retrieved December 9, 2012 (http://education
-portal.com/occupational_therapy_assistant
_training.html).

ExploreHealthCareers.org. "Physical Therapist Assistant."
January 16, 2013. Retrieved January 21, 2013
(http://explorehealthcareers.org/en/Career/9/
Physical_Therapist_Assistant).

Henry Ford Community College. "Physical Therapist
Assistant." December 4, 2012. Retrieved December
9, 2012 (https://my.hfcc.edu/site_manager/
catalog_manager/programs/view_program
.asp?id=4164&view=s&showprinticon=y).

Medical Transcription Samples. "Physical Therapy
    Evaluation Medical Transcription Sample Reports."
    2012. Retrieved January 18, 2013 (https://sites
    .google.com/site/medicaltranscriptionsamples/
    physical-therapy-evaluation-medical-transcription
    -sample-report).
Occupational-Therapy-Degree.com. "Equipment and
    Techniques Occupational Therapists Use." 2013.
    Retrieved January 21, 2013 (http://www
    .occupational-therapy-degree.com/equipment
    -and-techniques-occupational-therapists-use).
O*NET OnLine. "Summary Report for: 31-2011.00—
    Occupational Therapy Assistants." 2010. Retrieved
    January 21, 2013 (http://www.onetonline.org/link/
    summary/31-2011.00).
O*NET OnLine. "Summary Report for: 31-2012.00—
    Occupational Therapy Aides." 2012. Retrieved
    December 16, 2012 (http://www.onetonline.org/
    link/summary/31-2012.00).
O*NET OnLine. "Summary Report for: 31-2021.00—
    Physical Therapist Assistants." 2010. Retrieved
    December 16, 2012 (http://www.onetonline.org/
    link/summary/31-2021.00).
O*NET OnLine. "Summary Report for: 31-2022.00—
    Physical Therapist Aides." 2010. Retrieved December
    9, 2012 (http://www.onetonline.org/link/
    summary/31-2022.00).
SunsetBeach.com. "Common Types of Physical Therapy
    Equipment." Retrieved January 18, 2013 (http://
    www.sunsetbeach.com/story/Common-Types-of
    -Physical-Therapy-equipment/820232).

U.S. Bureau of Labor Statistics. "Occupational Therapy
    Assistants and Aides." *Occupational Outlook
    Handbook*, April 6, 2012. Retrieved December 9,
    2012 (http://www.bls.gov/ooh/healthcare/
    occupational-therapy-assistants-and-aides.htm).
U.S. Bureau of Labor Statistics. "Physical Therapy
    Assistants and Aides." *Occupational Outlook
    Handbook*, March 29, 2012. Retrieved December 9,
    2012 (http://www.bls.gov/ooh/healthcare/
    physical-therapist-assistants-and-aides.htm).

INDEX

A

accreditation, 28, 49
acute care, 17
American Occupational Therapy Association (AOTA), 39, 53, 64
American Physical Therapy Association (APTA), 64
American Speech-Language-Hearing Association (ASHA), 9
analytical listening, 32
attentive listening, 34

C

cardiovascular rehabilitation, 19
Certified Occupational Therapy Assistant (COTA) exam, 55
compassion, importance of, 31, 55
courteous listening, 34

D

directed listening, 34
Dreeben-Irimia, Olga, 32
dress codes, 60–61

G

geriatric care, 17, 19

H

home care, 22, 47

I

IEP (individual education program), 20–22
internships, 31

L

listening, importance of, 32, 35

N

National Physical Therapy Examination (NPTE), 34
neurological physical therapy, 19
nonverbal communication, 34, 35

O

occupational therapy
  general overview, 8–10, 39
  tools used, 43–45
occupational therapy aide, 10, 15, 38
occupational therapy assistant
  as bridge to becoming a therapist, 14–15, 56
  education/training, 48–53
  job outlook, 52

About the Author

Marcia Amidon Lusted is the author of more than 75 books and 350 magazine articles for young readers. She is also an assistant editor for Cobblestone Publishing, a writing instructor, and a musician. She recently completed eight weeks of physical therapy for a shoulder injury and observed the work of physical therapy students and assistants firsthand.

Photo Credits

Cover (patient and therapist) Glow Wellness/Getty Images; cover and interior pages (gym equipment) © iStockphoto.com/Sisoje; cover, back cover, p. 1 (background pattern) HunThomas/Shutterstock.com; pp. 4–5 (background) sfam_photo/Shutterstock.com; pp. 5 (inset), 26 Comstock/Thinkstock; p. 8 Tetra Images/Getty Images; p. 11 © iStockphoto.com/fatihhoca; p. 12 Tyler Olson/Shutterstock.com; p. 17 Larry Mulvehill/Photo Researchers/Getty Images; p. 18 Keith Brodsky/Digital Vision/Thinkstock; pp. 20–21 Tina Stallard/The Image Bank/Getty Images; p. 24, 61 Anderson Ross/Digital Vision/Getty Images; p. 30 PhotoAlto/Frederic Cirou/the Agency Collection/Getty Images; p. 33 Hemera Technologies/AbleStock.com/Thinkstock; p. 36 Roy Mehta/Riser/Getty Images; p. 40 The American Occupational Therapy Association; pp. 42–43 Image Source/Getty Images; p. 46 © AP Images; pp. 49, 54 Design Pics/Don Hammond/Getty Images; p. 51 Kim Gunkel/E+/Getty Images; pp. 58–59 Seth Joel/Photographer's Choice/Getty Images; p. 61 Anderson Ross/Digital Vision/Getty Images; p. 65 Fuse/Thinkstock.

Designer: Michael Moy; Editor: Andrea Sclarow Paskoff; Photo Researcher: Marty Levick